JOIE WARNER'S CAESAR SALADS

joie warner's

caesar salads

america's favorite salad

DESIGNED AND PHOTOGRAPHED BY

DREW WARNER

HEARST BOOKS
New York

a

flavor

book

Library of Congress Cataloging-in-Publication Data
Warner, Joie.
Joie Warner's Caesar salads: America's favorite salad /
by Joie Warner; photographs by Drew Warner.
p.   cm.
ISBN 0-688-12809-2
1. Salads.   I. Title.   II. Title: Caesar salads.
TX807.W36   1994
641.8'3—dc20   93-41264
CIP
Printed in Singapore   10 9 8 7 6 5 4 3 2 1

This book was created and produced by
Flavor Publications, Inc.
208 East 51st Street, Suite 240
New York, New York   10022

FIRST EDITION

A VERY SPECIAL THANKS to my husband Drew who does so many things so well. I would also like to thank Margaret Jackson for her fine editing. Thanks, too, to Tony Schroeter for his typesetting and especially for catching the things all the other eyes had missed.

CONTENTS

RECIPES

TAKE A BUNCH of romaine lettuce and some crispy croutons—make a deliciously tangy dressing with olive oil and a squeeze of lemon, a few cloves of garlic, a couple of dashes of Worcestershire sauce, some anchovies (or not, as you please) and mustard—then toss everything together with grated Parmesan cheese and what have you got? Caesar salad—the undisputed champion of greens and the most popular salad ever created.

By now you've probably heard the time-honored story of how the Italian restaurateur—Caesar Cardini— invented his south-of-the-border salad in Tijuana during Prohibition. How Hollywood movie stars were the first to venture down to Mr Cardini's café, coming in droves to do some serious drinking—and eating. When too many late-night patrons arrived one Fourth of July weekend, the restaurant ran out of food. Cardini frantically looked around to see what ingredients his restaurant had on hand. Locating several crates of romaine lettuce, he tossed the leaves with some excellent olive oil and eggs (which he first coddled) that he discovered in the storeroom. He sprinkled the

lettuce with salt and pepper, added a splash of fresh
lemon juice and Worcestershire sauce, and tumbled it
all with a generous grating of Parmesan cheese and
garlic-flavored croutons prepared with bread left over
from dinner. Thus his wondrous tableside salad was
born and, as they say, the rest is history!

The lusty Caesar was an immediate hit and soon
thereafter, the fame of Caesar's salad spread.
Californian chefs and restaurateurs immediately began
trying to duplicate his invention. Many believe that it
was during this time that anchovies—which Caesar
himself never used—made their way into recipes. And
although the salad craze started south of the American
border, it quickly became a celebrated California
creation. Nowadays Caesar salad is known worldwide as
an American classic and the top-selling greens are
featured on restaurant menus everywhere.

I fell in love with Caesar salad over twenty-five
years ago (as did my husband, Drew) and I've been
happily tossing and serving it to family and friends ever
since. This, then, is my ode to Caesar—for, in my
opinion, it is the most exciting, most exuberantly-
flavored, most deeply-satisfying salad ever devised. And
although Mr. Cardini might not have approved (he was
a purist, or so I've heard), my highly-personal recipes
have jazzed-up his original formula a bit and added
some new twists, ranging from sun-dried tomatoes to

crispy deep-fried calamari or zippy horseradish, and even pasta. Of course, I have included a close facsimile of the classic recipe which incorporates raw eggs. But I've taken the liberty of omitting eggs in my other recipes for both ease of preparation and safety (some regions have a problem with salmonella) and have substituted mayonnaise in several recipes to help the dressing cling to the leaves. And, while there are two schools of thought on seasoning—one says that the salad should be subtle, the other that it should be full-flavored (I'm of the full-flavored school)—my recipes are easily transformed into less pungent renditions by simply using less garlic, lemon, and anchovies (or no anchovies—if you absolutely must!).

I've enjoyed experimenting with each and every combination I could imagine and I hope you, too, will have fun making them and inventing your own Caesar salads. What is most important is that my creations please you as much as they have pleased my friends, my family, and me.

JOIE WARNER

10 SECRETS TO A
SUPREME CAESAR

1 First of all, start with impeccably fresh greens, avoiding any that are wilted or have yellowing leaves. Separate the leaves, then rinse each one well under cold running water. Thoroughly pat dry with paper towels, then break them into bite-size pieces—or break into bite-size pieces and then spin dry. (If the greens aren't dry, the dressing won't cling to the leaves and the moisture will adulterate the flavor.) Place in a plastic bag, then seal, and refrigerate for at least one hour to crisp.

2 Caesar salad connoisseurs chill their dinner plates (Caesars are always served in generous portions, piled high on dinner—not salad—plates: after all, most Caesars are complete meals in themselves), and many go as far as chilling the salad bowl and salad servers—even the knives and forks!

3 Always use quality olive oil (light but fragrant) and be sure it's fresh—olive oil does turn rancid. Choose excellent red wine or tarragon vinegar,

likewise, mustard. (I prefer wholegrain—also called
grainy or coarse grain—for the attractive look the
whole mustard seeds give. Dijon-type mustard is my
second choice.) Fresh, plump garlic cloves are essential,
as is freshly squeezed lemon juice—just the freshest
ingredients you can find.

4 Purchase Parmesan cheese freshly cut (not
pre-wrapped) from a quality cheese shop or
Italian grocer. Accept none other than Parmigiano
Reggiano—the name is stamped on the rind. Grate it
fresh yourself as you need it: a 1-ounce piece will yield
about ¼ cup grated, 2 ounces about ½ cup, and
3 ounces about ¾ cup.

5 Avoid store-bought croutons, homemade are
far superior in taste and so easy to make. Mix
and match any kind you wish from the crouton section:
those indicated in my recipes are merely suggestions.
French bread (see Croutons page 59) may be used
instead of white bread in crouton recipes.

6 If you wish to substitute anchovy paste for
canned fillets, about 1 tablespoon paste is the
equivalent of a 2-ounce can of fillets, but be careful:
anchovy pastes can be saltier than fillets so never add a
tablespoon all at once. Instead, add a teaspoon and
keep adding to taste. If you omit anchovies altogether,
you might want to add a little more Worcestershire
sauce for a flavor boost. (Though I've found most

people who don't care for anchovies still love Caesar
salad—anchovies and all—once they are mixed in!)

7 Most—but not all—of the dressings can be
made in a blender or food processor. If a
recipe doesn't specify a blender or food processor, then
it must be whisked in a bowl to preserve the texture of
the ingredients. If using a blender or processor, do not
purée the anchovies along with the ingredients if you
prefer a light-colored dressing; the puréed anchovies
turn it dark. Instead, stir in the chopped anchovies
after blending. Also, if using a whisk, be sure to blend
the mixture until emulsified—that is, lightly thickened
and bound together—(which is much quicker to
accomplish in a blender or processor) or the dressing
will separate and be oily. If the dressing is made ahead
and refrigerated, bring it to room temperature and
rewhisk or blend it if necessary before tossing with
the salad.

8 It is difficult to give the exact ratio of dressing
to greens. Add just enough dressing to coat the
salad lightly but thoroughly—overdressing is another
cause of limp and soggy greens. The amount of dressing
I provide in my recipes is for a large head of romaine.
I recommend you not add all of the dressing all at
once. Instead, add half, toss, then add more dressing to
taste. If you wish to reduce calories and fat, you may
find that half the dressing is just enough.

9 Use an extra-large bowl for tossing your salad (I use a 16-inch diameter stainless-steel bowl purchased from a restaurant supply or specialty cookware shop), then transfer the salad to individual chilled plates or to a smaller, more attractive (and preferably chilled) salad bowl.

10 All the various salad components can be prepared well ahead of time, but the salad must be tossed at the last minute to ensure the greens stay crisp. If tossed ahead of time and allowed to sit, the salt in the dressing will cause the greens to wilt.

CLASSIC CAESAR SALAD

t*o my mind, a Caesar just isn't a Caesar without the gutsy excitement of anchovies. But what many don't realize is that the original salad didn't contain anchovies—or mustard for that matter. These embellishments were added some time later by cooks unknown. The following recipe is a close facsimile of Chef Caesar Cardini's invention. Modern cooks can whip up the dressing in a blender or food processor if desired.*

3 large garlic cloves, peeled, crushed with flat side of knife
½ cup olive oil
1 large head romaine lettuce, rinsed, dried, broken into bite-size pieces
Salt and freshly ground black pepper
1 large lemon, halved
Worcestershire sauce
1 large raw egg, or coddled egg (boiled for exactly 1 minute)
1 can (2 ounces) anchovy fillets, drained, chopped (optional)
½ cup freshly grated Parmesan cheese, plus extra for serving
1½ cups Garlic Croutons (page 60)

Combine garlic and oil and let stand for a minimum of 1 hour, preferably overnight. ❧ Crisp lettuce: place in plastic bag, seal, and refrigerate for a minimum of 1 hour. ❧ Toss crisped lettuce in very large salad bowl with oil (discarding garlic) until thoroughly coated. Sprinkle with a little salt and add several grinds black pepper. Squeeze lemon to taste over greens, add several dashes of Worcestershire sauce, and break egg over top; toss again. Sprinkle with anchovies if using, cheese, and croutons and toss until combined. Serve with extra cheese and pass the peppermill.

SERVES 6.

Note: In many regions it is not advisable to use raw or coddled eggs because of salmonella contamination. Simply omit the egg, or substitute 2 tablespoons mayonnaise if you wish.

CREAMY CAESAR SALAD

m ade with bottled mayonnaise, this exquisitely rich dressing is one of the easiest Caesar salads I know.

1 large head romaine lettuce, rinsed, dried, broken
  into bite-size pieces
1 large garlic clove, finely chopped
1 tablespoon anchovy paste
¼ cup fresh lemon juice
1 tablespoon wholegrain or Dijon mustard
1 teaspoon Worcestershire sauce
1 cup mayonnaise
½ cup freshly grated Parmesan cheese, plus extra
  for serving
1 cup Pumpernickel Croutons (page 62)

Crisp lettuce: place in plastic bag, seal, and refrigerate for a
minimum of 1 hour. ❧ Whisk garlic, anchovy paste, lemon juice,
mustard, and Worcestershire sauce in medium bowl until blended.
Add mayonnaise and cheese and whisk until smooth. Cover and
chill for several hours. ❧ Toss crisped lettuce in very large salad
bowl with dressing until thoroughly coated. Add croutons and
toss again. Serve with extra cheese.

SERVES 6.

CAESAR SALAD WITH HORSERADISH

h *orseradish gives this salad a definitive bite: be sure to taste as you go—not all horseradishes are created equal!*

1 large head romaine lettuce, rinsed, dried, broken
   into bite-size pieces
3 garlic cloves, finely chopped
1 can (2 ounces) anchovy fillets, drained, chopped
4 tablespoons red wine vinegar
2 tablespoons mayonnaise
½ teaspoon dry mustard
1 teaspoon Worcestershire sauce
2 tablespoons drained bottled extra-hot horseradish,
   or to taste
½ cup olive oil
½ cup freshly grated Parmesan, plus extra for serving
1½ cups Croutons or Bagel Croutons (page 59, 62)

Crisp lettuce: place in plastic bag, seal, and refrigerate for a
minimum of 1 hour. ∾ Whisk garlic, anchovies, vinegar,
mayonnaise, mustard, Worcestershire sauce, and horseradish in
medium bowl until blended (or blend in blender or food
processor). Continue whisking or blending while adding oil in
thin stream until thickened. Blend in cheese. Cover and chill for
several hours if desired; reblend if necessary. ∾ Toss crisped
lettuce in very large salad bowl with dressing until thoroughly
coated. Add croutons and toss again. Serve with extra cheese.

SERVES 6.

QUICK AND EASY CAESAR SALAD

*d*eliciously assertive, this is my standard Caesar salad. As I mentioned earlier, for anyone shy of anchovies, lemon, or garlic, this recipe—or any of those that follow—can simply be adjusted to taste. Full-flavor fans—like me—will enjoy it just as is.

 1 large head romaine lettuce, rinsed, dried, broken
    into bite-size pieces
 3 large garlic cloves
 1 can (2 ounces) anchovy fillets, drained
 1 tablespoon wholegrain or Dijon mustard
 ¼ cup fresh lemon juice
 1 teaspoon Worcestershire sauce
 ½ cup olive oil
 ½ cup freshly grated Parmesan cheese, plus extra
    for serving
 1½ cups Pumpernickel Croutons (page 62)

Crisp lettuce: place in plastic bag, seal, and refrigerate for a minimum of 1 hour. ❧ Chop garlic, then anchovies in food processor. Add mustard, lemon juice, and Worcestershire sauce and whirl until blended. (Or blend finely chopped garlic and anchovies with seasonings in blender.) Continue blending while adding oil in thin stream until thickened. Blend in cheese. Cover and chill for several hours if desired; reblend if necessary. ❧ Toss crisped lettuce in very large salad bowl with dressing until thoroughly coated. Add croutons and toss again. Serve with extra cheese.

SERVES 6.

BLUE CHEESE CAESAR SALAD

b *lue cheese is an exceptional complement to a Caesar and it's a variation I'm particularly fond of. For a creamier version, simply prepare the dressing in a blender or food processor using all of the blue cheese and blending until smooth. If you wish, you may also add a sprinkling of Bacon Bits (page 63) on top.*

1 large head romaine lettuce, rinsed, dried, broken
   into bite-size pieces
1 large garlic clove, finely chopped
1 can (2 ounces) anchovy fillets, drained, chopped
3 tablespoons fresh lemon juice
1 teaspoon Worcestershire sauce
⅓ cup mayonnaise
⅔ cup crumbled blue cheese
½ cup olive oil
1½ cups Pumpernickel Croutons (page 62)
   Freshly grated Parmesan cheese

Crisp lettuce: place in plastic bag, seal, and refrigerate for a minimum of 1 hour. ∾ Whisk garlic, anchovies, lemon juice, Worcestershire sauce, mayonnaise, and half the blue cheese in medium bowl until blended. Continue whisking while adding oil in thin stream until thickened. Cover and chill for several hours if desired; reblend if necessary. ∾ Toss crisped lettuce in very large salad bowl with dressing until thoroughly coated. Add croutons and remaining blue cheese and toss again. Serve with Parmesan cheese.

SERVES 6.

MEXICAN CAESAR WITH PARMESAN
TORTILLA CROUTONS

*arried to a marvelous Mexican mixture of lime
juice, tomatoes, avocado, and tortilla croutons—*
I believe this to be one of the most charming Caesars ever tossed.

1 large head romaine lettuce, rinsed, dried, broken
into bite-size pieces

3 garlic cloves, finely chopped

1 can (2 ounces) anchovy fillets, drained, chopped

1 tablespoon wholegrain or Dijon mustard

¼ cup fresh lime juice

½ cup olive oil

½ cup freshly grated Parmesan cheese, plus extra
for serving

2 large ripe plum tomatoes, seeded, chopped

1 avocado, peeled, pitted, cubed just before using
Parmesan Tortilla Croutons (page 63)

Crisp lettuce: place in plastic bag, seal, and refrigerate for a
minimum of 1 hour. ∾ Whisk garlic, anchovies, mustard, and
lime juice in medium bowl until blended (or blend in blender or
food processor). Continue whisking or blending while adding oil
in thin stream until thickened. Stir in cheese and tomatoes; set
aside to marinate tomatoes for a minimum of 1 hour, or cover
and chill for several hours; restir if necessary. ∾ Toss crisped
lettuce in very large salad bowl with dressing until thoroughly
coated. Add avocado and tortilla croutons and toss again. Serve
with extra cheese.

SERVES 6.

C A E S A R   S A L A D S

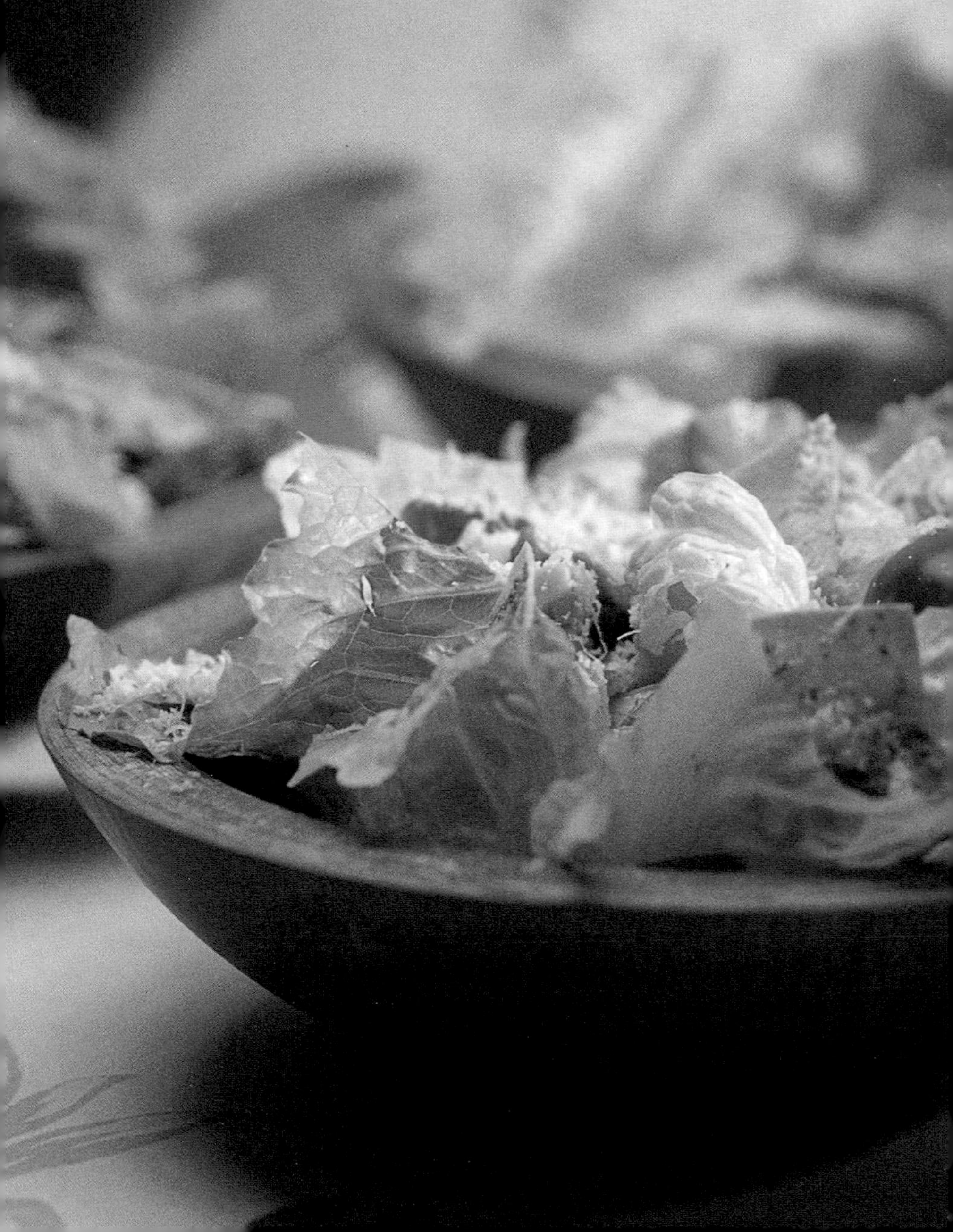

SEAFOOD CAESAR SALAD

e ndowed with luscious crab and shrimp, this is one of Caesar's most luxurious unions. You might want to try fresh—not frozen—scallops and lobster meat.

½ pound raw shrimp, unpeeled
1 large head romaine lettuce, rinsed, dried, broken into bite-size pieces
3 garlic cloves, finely chopped
4 anchovy fillets, chopped
1 tablespoon wholegrain or Dijon mustard
¼ cup fresh lemon juice
1 teaspoon Worcestershire sauce
½ teaspoon Tabasco sauce (optional)
½ cup olive oil
½ cup freshly grated Parmesan cheese, plus extra for serving
½ pound crabmeat, if frozen, thawed, squeezed dry, picked over
Grated zest of 1 medium lemon
1½ cups Cayenne Croutons (page 60)

Cook shrimp in saucepan of boiling salted water for 1 to 2 minutes or just until cooked through. Drain, cool under cold running water, and peel. Cover and chill before using. ❧ Crisp lettuce: place in plastic bag, seal, and refrigerate for a minimum of 1 hour. ❧ Whisk garlic, anchovies, mustard, lemon juice, Worcestershire and Tabasco sauces in medium bowl until blended (or blend in blender or food processor). Continue whisking or blending while adding oil in thin stream until thickened.

Blend in cheese. Cover and chill for several hours if desired; reblend if necessary. ✆ Toss crisped lettuce in very large salad bowl with dressing until thoroughly coated. Add shrimp, crabmeat, lemon zest, and croutons and toss again. Serve with extra cheese.

SERVES 6.

photo overleaf ☛

CAESAR SALAD WITH
SMOKED SALMON

moked salmon, capers, and red onion add a tempting new twist—and a touch of elegance—to a Caesar salad. Try it—it's absolutely spectacular! If fresh tarragon is nowhere to be found, you may just omit it.

1 large head romaine lettuce, rinsed, dried, broken into bite-size pieces
2 large garlic cloves, finely chopped
1 can (2 ounces) anchovy fillets, drained, chopped
2 tablespoons tarragon vinegar
1 tablespoon wholegrain or Dijon mustard
1 teaspoon Worcestershire sauce
2 tablespoons mayonnaise
½ cup olive oil
2 tablespoons freshly grated Parmesan cheese, plus extra for serving
¾ pound thinly sliced smoked salmon, cut into 1-inch pieces
2 tablespoons coarsely chopped fresh tarragon leaves
1 generous tablespoon drained capers
Several very thin slices red onion, rings separated
1½ cups Pumpernickel Croutons (page 62)

Crisp lettuce: place in plastic bag, seal, and refrigerate for a minimum of 1 hour. ∾ Whisk garlic, anchovies, vinegar, mustard, Worcestershire sauce, and mayonnaise in medium bowl until blended (or blend in blender or food processor).

Continue whisking or blending while adding oil in thin stream
until thickened. Blend in cheese. Cover and chill for several hours
if desired; reblend if necessary. ❧ Toss crisped lettuce in very
large salad bowl with dressing until thoroughly coated. Add
salmon, tarragon, capers, onion, and croutons and toss again.
Serve with extra cheese.

SERVES 6.

MANY GREENS CAESAR SALAD

a n updated alternative to the usual romaine lettuce.

1 large head Boston lettuce, rinsed, dried, broken into
  bite-size pieces
1 bunch arugula, rinsed, dried, tough stems removed
1 small bunch watercress, rinsed, dried, tough stems
  removed
2 large garlic cloves, finely chopped
1 can (2 ounces) anchovy fillets, drained, chopped
2 generous tablespoons chopped fresh tarragon
½ teaspoon dry mustard
½ teaspoon Worcestershire sauce
¼ cup fresh lemon juice
½ cup olive oil
½ cup freshly grated Parmesan cheese, plus extra
  for serving
  Several very thin slices red onion, rings separated
1½ cups Croutons or Garlic Croutons (page 59, 60)

Crisp greens: place in plastic bags, seal, and refrigerate for a
minimum of 1 hour. ∾ Whisk garlic, anchovies, tarragon,
mustard, Worcestershire sauce, and lemon juice in medium bowl
until blended. Continue whisking while adding oil in thin stream
until thickened. Blend in cheese and stir in onion. Set aside to
marinate onion for a minimum of 1 hour; restir if necessary. ∾
Toss crisped greens in very large salad bowl with dressing until
thoroughly coated. Add croutons and toss again. Serve with extra
cheese and pass the peppermill.

SERVES 4 TO 6.

CAESAR SALAD WITH RADICCHIO

r *adicchio paired with romaine lettuce makes a sharp-tasting, vividly-colored Caesar.*

1 medium head romaine lettuce, rinsed, dried, broken
into bite-size pieces
1 can (2 ounces) anchovy fillets, drained, reserving oil,
chopped
3 garlic cloves, finely chopped
¼ cup fresh lemon juice
1 tablespoon wholegrain or Dijon mustard
1 teaspoon Worcestershire sauce
½ teaspoon sugar
½ cup olive oil
½ cup freshly grated Parmesan cheese, plus extra
for serving
1 to 2 cups bite-size pieces radicchio
1½ cups Pumpernickel or Parmesan Croutons (page 62, 59)

Crisp lettuce: place in plastic bag, seal, and refrigerate for a
minimum of 1 hour. ∾ Whisk anchovies, garlic, lemon juice,
mustard, Worcestershire sauce, and sugar in medium bowl until
blended (or blend in blender or food processor). Continue
whisking or blending while adding olive and anchovy oils in thin
stream until thickened. Blend in cheese. Cover and chill for
several hours if desired; reblend if necessary. ∾ Toss crisped
lettuce and radicchio in very large salad bowl with dressing until
thoroughly coated. Add croutons and toss again. Serve with
extra cheese.

SERVES 6.

photo overleaf ☞

CAESAR SALAD WITH
GRILLED SWORDFISH

S *wordfish seems to be the current rage—and that it partners perfectly with Caesar is not surprising.*

1 large head romaine lettuce, rinsed, dried, broken into bite-size pieces
3 garlic cloves, finely chopped
1 can (2 ounces) anchovy fillets, drained, chopped
¼ cup fresh lemon juice
1 tablespoon wholegrain or Dijon mustard
1 teaspoon Worcestershire sauce
1 tablespoon mayonnaise
½ cup olive oil
1 pound swordfish steaks
½ cup freshly grated Parmesan cheese, plus extra for serving
2 tablespoons drained capers
Several very thin slices red onion, rings separated
1½ cups Croutons or Parmesan Croutons (page 59)

Crisp lettuce: place in plastic bag, seal, and refrigerate for a minimum of 1 hour. ∾ Whisk garlic, anchovies, lemon juice, mustard, Worcestershire sauce, and mayonnaise in medium bowl until blended (or blend in blender or food processor). Continue whisking or blending while adding oil in thin stream until thickened. Cover and chill for several hours if desired; reblend if necessary. ∾ Prepare grill. Place swordfish on grill and cook for 3 minutes each side, basting with 2 tablespoons dressing, until seared on the outside and just cooked through.

Transfer to cutting surface; cut into 1-inch pieces and keep warm.
➣ Blend cheese into dressing. Toss crisped lettuce in very large
salad bowl with dressing until thoroughly coated. Add swordfish,
capers, onion, and croutons and gently toss again. Serve with
extra cheese.

SERVES 6.

CAESAR SALAD WITH FRIED
OYSTERS AND CALAMARI

O ysters and squid (a.k.a. its more poetic Italian name, calamari) are deep-fried until crispy golden, then nestled in lemony-tart, leafy greens. This heavenly Caesar is so spectacular that, whenever I serve it, my guests swoon with delight!

1 large head romaine lettuce, rinsed, dried, broken into
  bite-size pieces
3 garlic cloves, finely chopped
1 can (2 ounces) anchovy fillets, drained, chopped
1 tablespoon wholegrain or Dijon mustard
  Grated zest of 1 small lemon
¼ cup fresh lemon juice
  Freshly ground black pepper
½ cup olive oil
½ cup freshly grated Parmesan cheese, plus extra
  for serving
  About ¾ cup all-purpose flour
  About ½ cup fine dry breadcrumbs
1 large egg beaten with 2 tablespoons milk
1½ pounds medium-small squid, cleaned, bodies cut
  into ¼-inch rings, tentacles left whole, patted dry
18 shucked oysters, well drained
  Vegetable oil for frying
  Salt

Crisp lettuce: place in plastic bag, seal, and refrigerate for a minimum of 1 hour. ᐯ Whisk garlic, anchovies, mustard, lemon zest, lemon juice, and pepper in medium bowl until blended. Continue whisking while adding oil in thin stream until thickened. Blend in cheese. Cover and chill for several hours if desired; rewhisk if necessary. ᐯ Place flour and breadcrumbs on 2 separate pieces of wax paper. Beat egg and milk in small bowl. Coat squid lightly with flour, then set on baking sheet in single layer. Coat oysters lightly with flour; dip in egg mixture, allowing excess to drain, then coat with breadcrumbs. Place in single layer on another baking sheet. (You may refrigerate squid and oysters for up to one hour before cooking.) ᐯ In deep large, heavy skillet, heat about 1½ inches oil over high heat to 360°F. Fry squid in batches (covering skillet with spatter screen: squid has a tendency to splatter while frying) for 1 minute or just until crisp and pale golden—no longer; remove, with slotted spoon, to paper towels to drain and sprinkle with salt. Fry oysters in batches for several seconds each side or until crisp and golden; remove to paper towels to drain and sprinkle with salt. ᐯ Immediately toss crisped lettuce in very large salad bowl with dressing until thoroughly coated. Divide among chilled dinner plates and top with just-fried oysters and calamari. Serve with extra cheese.

SERVES 6.

photo overleaf ☞

CAESAR POTATO SALAD

P otatoes are pampered with a piquant blend of bold
Caesar dressing and sweet sun-dried tomatoes—
a wonderful idea for your next summer picnic
or backyard barbecue.

2 pounds (4 large) red potatoes, unpeeled, cubed
1 large garlic clove, finely chopped
¼ cup olive oil
¼ cup red wine vinegar
1 tablespoon wholegrain or Dijon mustard
1 teaspoon salt
  Freshly ground black pepper
4 anchovy fillets, chopped
10 to 12 large halves sun-dried tomatoes in oil,
   drained, diced
¼ cup diced red onion
2 tablespoons freshly grated Parmesan cheese
2 tablespoons chopped fresh flat-leaf parsley

Drop potatoes into saucepan of boiling water and cook for
8 minutes or until tender; drain well and cool slightly. ❧ Whisk
garlic, oil, vinegar, mustard, salt and pepper in large bowl until
blended. Add potatoes, anchovies, sun-dried tomatoes, red onion,
cheese, and parsley; stir gently to thoroughly combine. Serve
warm or at room temperature.

SERVES 6.

CAESAR SALAD WITH WARM
BACON DRESSING

f Chef Cardini had been French, I suspect he might have composed his Caesar salad just like this.

4 thick slices best-quality bacon, cut into
½-inch pieces
About 3 tablespoons olive oil
8 cups bite-size pieces romaine lettuce, rinsed,
dried, chilled
4 anchovy fillets, chopped
½ cup Herb or Cayenne Croutons (page 59, 60)
1 tablespoon wholegrain or Dijon mustard
1 tablespoon red wine vinegar
A small wedge Parmesan cheese

Cook bacon in nonstick medium skillet over medium-high heat until crisp. Remove to paper-towel-lined plate to drain, reserving bacon fat. Measure amount of fat and add enough olive oil to make ¼ cup. ∾ Divide crisped lettuce among four dinner plates and sprinkle with anchovies, croutons, and bacon. ∾ Stir oil mixture, mustard, and vinegar in skillet and heat just until warm-hot—not sizzling hot. Spoon oil mixture equally over salads. Using vegetable peeler, shave cheese into several wide thin strips and arrange over salad. Serve at once.

SERVES 4.

CAESAR PASTA SALAD

or a hearty Caesar with a difference, here's an alliance of pasta and Caesar that's really quite toothsome. Once tossed, the salad must be served promptly, but all other preparations can be done several hours ahead.

½ pound fusilli
2 large garlic cloves, finely chopped
1 can (2 ounces) anchovy fillets, drained, chopped
1 tablespoon wholegrain or Dijon mustard
¼ cup fresh lemon juice
¼ cup chopped fresh basil leaves
½ cup olive oil
¾ cup freshly grated Parmesan cheese
   Freshly ground black pepper
8 cups bite-size pieces romaine lettuce, rinsed,
   dried, chilled
1 small sweet red pepper, seeded, diced
1 cup Croutons or Herb Croutons (page 59)

Cook pasta in large pot of boiling salted water until *al dente*; drain, rinse under cold running water, and drain well again. Toss with a little oil to keep pasta from sticking together, then cover and chill. ∾ Whisk garlic, anchovies, mustard, lemon juice, and basil in medium bowl until blended. Continue whisking while adding oil in thin stream until thickened. Cover and chill dressing. ∾ Just before serving, toss pasta, dressing, cheese, and pepper in large bowl. Add lettuce, red pepper, and croutons and toss again.

SERVES 6.

photo overleaf ☞

CAESAR SALAD WITH SUN-
DRIED TOMATOES

*just couldn't resist adding sun-dried tomatoes to my
Caesar dressing. The result is—to say the least—
truly beguiling. Be sure to use only best-quality
sun-dried tomatoes that are bright red—not brown.*

 1 large head romaine lettuce, rinsed, dried, broken
 into bite-size pieces
 2 large garlic cloves, finely chopped
 1 can (2 ounces) anchovy fillets, drained, chopped
 1 tablespoon wholegrain or Dijon mustard
 3 tablespoons fresh lemon juice
 1 tablespoon red wine vinegar
 ½ cup olive oil
 10 large halves sun-dried tomatoes in oil, drained, diced
 ½ cup freshly grated Parmesan cheese, plus extra for
 serving
 1½ cups Pumpernickel or Parmesan Croutons (page 62, 59)

Crisp lettuce: place in plastic bag, seal, and refrigerate for a
minimum of 1 hour. ∿ Whisk garlic, anchovies, mustard, lemon
juice, and vinegar in medium bowl until blended (or blend in
blender or food processor). Continue whisking or blending while
adding oil in thin stream until thickened. Stir in sun-dried
tomatoes and cheese. Cover and chill for several hours if desired;
restir if necessary. ∿ Toss crisped lettuce in very large salad
bowl with dressing until thoroughly coated. Add croutons and
toss again. Serve with extra cheese.

SERVES 6.

CAESAR SALAD WITH
GRILLED CHICKEN

ust before serving, grill or broil the chicken—everything else can be prepared ahead of time, then tossed together at the last minute. Alternatively, you may use steak (about ¾ pound), omitting the oil and lemon marinade and generously coating it with cracked pepper before grilling, then cut into thin slices.

1   large head romaine lettuce, rinsed, dried, broken
    into bite-size pieces
3   garlic cloves, finely chopped
1   can (2 ounces) anchovy fillets, chopped
1   tablespoon wholegrain or Dijon mustard
1   tablespoon mayonnaise
¼   cup fresh lemon juice
1   teaspoon Worcestershire sauce
½   cup olive oil
½   cup freshly grated Parmesan cheese, plus extra
    for serving
1   tablespoon olive oil
1   tablespoon fresh lemon juice
    Freshly ground black pepper
3   skinless, boneless chicken breast halves
½   pound ripe cherry tomatoes, thinly sliced
1½ cups Herb Croutons (page 59)

Crisp lettuce: place in plastic bag, seal, and refrigerate for a minimum of 1 hour. ❧ Whisk garlic, anchovies, mustard, mayonnaise, lemon juice, and Worcestershire sauce in medium bowl until blended (or blend in blender or food processor). Continue whisking or blending while adding oil in thin stream until thickened. Blend in cheese. Cover and chill for several hours if desired; reblend if necessary. ᖉ Combine oil, lemon juice, and pepper in glass pie plate. Add chicken and turn to coat evenly; set aside for 30 minutes to marinate. ᖉ Prepare grill or preheat broiler. Grill or broil chicken for 6 minutes each side or just until cooked through. Transfer to cutting surface; cut into bite-size pieces. ᖉ Toss crisped lettuce with dressing in very large salad bowl until thoroughly coated. Add chicken, tomatoes, and croutons and toss again. Serve with extra cheese and pass the peppermill.

SERVES 6.

FOUR-BEAN CAESAR SALAD

h*ere's how to take a nice-but-boring bean salad and give it a bright new tang. How? By spicing the beans with Caesar dressing, of course!*

½ pound fresh green beans, stem ends removed
½ pound fresh yellow beans, stem ends removed
1 can (19 ounces) garbanzo beans (chickpeas), drained, rinsed
1 can (19 ounces) kidney beans, drained, rinsed
1 large garlic clove, finely chopped
¼ cup finely diced red onion
Scant ⅓ cup fresh lemon juice
¼ cup olive oil
1 tablespoon wholegrain or Dijon mustard
About 1 teaspoon salt
Freshly ground black pepper
1 can (2 ounces) anchovy fillets, chopped

Blanch green and yellow beans in boiling water for 4 minutes or until tender but still brightly colored; drain, and plunge into ice water to chill, then drain again. Pat beans dry with paper towels; cut into thirds. ✍ Place green and yellow beans, garbanzo and kidney beans, garlic, onion, lemon juice, oil, mustard, salt to taste, and pepper in large bowl. Stir until combined, then add anchovies; stir again. Serve at room temperature or chilled.

S E R V E S 6 .

GREEK CAESAR WITH FETA, MINT, AND OLIVES

h ere I've joined the two most popular green salads
—Caesar and Greek—for a result that—I know
you'll agree—is truly fabulous.

1 large head romaine lettuce, rinsed, dried, broken
  into bite-size pieces
2 large garlic cloves, finely chopped
4 anchovy fillets, chopped
1 tablespoon wholegrain or Dijon mustard
1 teaspoon dried oregano
¼ cup fresh lemon juice
½ cup olive oil
2 large ripe plum tomatoes, seeded, coarsely chopped
  Several very thin slices red onion, rings separated
1 cup crumbled feta cheese
¼ cup freshly grated Parmesan cheese, plus extra for
  serving
½ cup Greek black olives (Kalamata), unpitted
¼ cup coarsely chopped fresh mint leaves
  Pita Croutons (page 62)

Crisp lettuce: place in plastic bag, seal, and refrigerate for a
minimum of 1 hour. ∾ Whisk garlic, anchovies, mustard,
oregano, and lemon juice in medium bowl until blended. Continue
whisking while adding oil in thin stream until thickened. Stir in
tomatoes, onions, feta and Parmesan cheese. Set aside to marinate
tomatoes and onions for a minimum of 1 hour, or cover

and chill for several hours; restir if necessary. ⌒ Toss crisped lettuce in very large salad bowl with dressing until thoroughly coated. Add olives, mint, and croutons and toss again. Serve with extra Parmesan cheese.

SERVES 6.

CAESAR COLE SLAW

What follows is not your typical cole slaw. Spiked with Caesar dressing, this rendition is admittedly zippy but absolutely scrumptious. You can make the dressing a few hours ahead of time (kept covered and chilled) but to be perfect, the cabbage should be sliced and tossed with the dressing no more than an hour before serving.

1   can (2 ounces) anchovy fillets, drained
1   large garlic clove, finely chopped
¼   cup fresh lemon juice
1   tablespoon wholegrain or Dijon mustard
1   teaspoon Worcestershire sauce
1   cup mayonnaise
½   cup freshly grated Parmesan cheese
1   medium head (2 pounds) green cabbage
1   large sweet red pepper, seeded, cut into julienne
    Salt and freshly ground black pepper

Finely chop, then mash to a paste 4 of the anchovies. Chop remaining anchovies and set aside. ℕ Whisk mashed anchovies, garlic, lemon juice, mustard, and Worcestershire sauce in medium bowl until combined. Add mayonnaise and cheese, whisking until smooth. Cover and chill if desired. ℕ Just before serving, remove and discard outer leaves of cabbage, cut in half, and core. Slice into roughly ¼-inch thick strips and place in very large bowl. Add red pepper and toss. Add dressing, along with chopped anchovies, salt, and pepper; toss to combine. Serve immediately or cover and chill for up to 1 hour.

SERVES 6 TO 8.

photo preceding page

CROUTONS

2 cups (1-inch cubes) French bread, with crusts,
   or (½-inch cubes) white bread, crusts removed
1½ tablespoons olive oil

Preheat oven to 400°F. Place bread cubes on baking sheet, drizzle
with oil, and toss to combine. Spread in single layer and bake for
10 minutes or until crisp and golden.

MAKES ABOUT 1½ CUPS.

PARMESAN CROUTONS

2 cups diced (½-inch cubes) white bread, crusts removed
1½ tablespoons olive oil
2 tablespoons freshly grated Parmesan cheese

Preheat oven to 400°F. Place bread cubes on baking sheet, drizzle
with oil, and toss to combine. Spread in single layer and bake for
10 minutes or until crisp and golden. Remove from oven and toss
with cheese.

MAKES ABOUT 1½ CUPS.

HERB CROUTONS

2 cups diced (½-inch cubes) white bread, crusts removed
1½ tablespoons olive oil
1 teaspoon dried oregano
1 teaspoon dried thyme
1 tablespoon freshly grated Parmesan cheese (optional)

Preheat oven to 400°F. Place bread cubes on baking sheet, drizzle

with oil, and toss to combine. Sprinkle with oregano and
thyme, toss again, and spread in single layer. Bake for 10 minutes
or until crisp and golden. Remove from oven and toss with
cheese if desired.

MAKES ABOUT 1½ CUPS.

CAYENNE CROUTONS

2 cups diced (½-inch cubes) white bread, crusts removed
1½ tablespoons olive oil
½ teaspoon cayenne

Preheat oven to 400°F. Place bread cubes on baking sheet, drizzle
with oil, and toss to combine. Sprinkle with cayenne, toss again,
and spread in single layer. Bake for 10 minutes or until crisp
and golden.

MAKES ABOUT 1½ CUPS.

GARLIC CROUTONS

2 cups diced (½-inch cubes) white bread, crusts removed
1½ tablespoons olive oil, or garlic-infused oil
  (see Classic Caesar Salad page 16)
1 medium garlic clove, minced

Preheat oven to 400°F. Place bread cubes on baking sheet, drizzle
with oil, and toss to combine; spread in single layer. (If using
garlic-infused oil, bake for 10 minutes or until crisp and golden.)
Bake for 5 minutes, remove from oven, and sprinkle with garlic.
Return to oven and bake another 5 minutes or until crisp and
golden.

MAKES ABOUT 1½ CUPS.

PITA CROUTONS

2 tablespoons olive oil
1 teaspoon dried oregano
2 (6-inch) pitas

Preheat broiler. ❧ Combine oil and oregano in small bowl; brush tops of pitas lightly with mixture. Using scissors or sharp knife, cut pitas into roughly 1-inch squares (you should have 2 cups); place oil side up on baking sheet. Place under broiler for 2 minutes or until crisp and golden.

MAKES ABOUT 2 CUPS.

PUMPERNICKEL CROUTONS

2 cups diced (½-inch cubes) pumpernickel (or dark rye) bread, crusts removed
1½ tablespoons olive oil
2 tablespoons freshly grated Parmesan cheese (optional)

Preheat oven to 400°F. Place bread cubes on baking sheet, drizzle with oil, and toss to combine. Spread in single layer and bake for 10 minutes or until crisp. Remove from oven and toss with cheese if desired.

MAKES ABOUT 1½ CUPS.

BAGEL CROUTONS

1 plain or onion bagel, sliced into thin rounds
2 tablespoons olive oil

Preheat oven to 400°F. Brush both sides of bagel rounds lightly with oil. Place on baking sheet in single layer and bake for 10 minutes or until crisp and golden.

MAKES ABOUT 1 ½ CUPS.

PARMESAN TORTILLA CROUTONS

- 5 corn tortillas
- 2 tablespoons olive oil
    Salt
- 2 tablespoons freshly grated Parmesan cheese

Preheat oven to 400°F. Brush both sides of tortillas lightly with oil and sprinkle one side with a little salt. Using scissors or sharp knife, cut tortillas into roughly 1-inch squares. Place squares slightly overlapping in single layer on baking sheet. Bake for 5 minutes or just until crisp; watch carefully. Sprinkle cheese over croutons and bake another minute or just until melted and golden—do not overcook.

BACON BITS

- 4 slices bacon, pancetta, or prosciutto, cut into
    ½-inch pieces

Cook bacon, pancetta, or prosciutto in nonstick skillet over medium-high heat until crisp. Using slotted spoon, transfer to paper towels to drain.